Jennie Robinson

The United States as a Third Party in the Civil War in Angola

GRIN Verlag

Bibliografische Information der Deutschen Nationalbibliothek:

Die Deutsche Bibliothek verzeichnet diese Publikation in der Deutschen National-
bibliografie; detaillierte bibliografische Daten sind im Internet über http://dnb.d-
nb.de/ abrufbar.

Imprint:

Copyright © 2006 GRIN Verlag GmbH
Druck und Bindung: Books on Demand GmbH, Norderstedt Germany
ISBN: 978-3-640-50018-5

This book at GRIN:

http://www.grin.com/en/e-book/135437/the-united-states-as-a-third-party-in-the-
civil-war-in-angola

University of Malta

Department of International Relations

Course: IRL 2097 Conflict Resolution

Assignment:

Question 2 - *By reference to a case study of your choice, discuss how third party intervention often render resolution of the conflict more difficult if the primary concern of the third party is its own narrow self-interest.*

'The United States as a Third Party in the Civil War in Angola'

Jennie Hery-Jaona

B.A. (Hons.) 2nd year

Deadline: May 12, 2006

Introduction

Angolan nationalist movements' struggle for independence (gained in 1975) against the Portuguese colonial power was to transform into an intrastate conflict between the parties: MPLA, backed by Cuba, and the FNLA plus Unita, backed by South Africa and the United States (US); and into an interstate conflict entangled within the Cold War scenario, so as to involve outsiders such as the Soviet Union, the US, Cuba and South Africa, each seeking to "shape an outcome that would advance its perceived interests".[1]

This paper will attempt to address the question of how third party intervention, in this case the US renders resolution of the conflict more difficult because of its primary concern being its own narrow self-interest.

Development

A. The role of a third party

According to Bercovitch and Houston, "the practice of settling disputes through intermediaries has a rich history in all cultures, both Western and non-Western". However, due to the nature of the international arena, "with its anarchical features of escalating conflicts, shrinking resources, rising ethnic demands, and the absence of generally accepted 'rules of the game', the potential application of mediation is truly unbounded".[2] As part of the conflict resolution process, a third party's entry can reflect "changes in the conflict structure and allows a different pattern of communications, enabling the third party to filter or reflect back the messages, attitudes and behaviour of the conflictants". Nonetheless, a third party can also change the power balance and even risks to find itself "sucked into the conflict as a full party" if it is powerful, i.e. in the case of politicians and governments. Miall et al. distinguish between "powerful mediators, who bring their power resources to bear, and powerless mediators, whose role is confined to communication and facilitation. Among the means used to "seek or force an outcome, typically along the win-lose or 'bargaining' line are: "good offices, mediation, and sticks and carrots". Still, in the case of asymmetric conflicts, which support a top dog-underdog structure, conflict resolution can

---

[1] D. Rothchild, Conflict management in Angola

only occur with the change of the structure, though this cannot be in the interests of the top dog. In the case of no win-win outcomes, the third party would join forces with the underdog so as to bring about a resolution. The role of the third party is on the whole to transform "what were unpeaceful, unbalanced relationships into peaceful and dynamic ones" and if required, encounter the top dog.[3] However, it also takes time to solve a conflict, and the civil war in Angola was to last more than twenty years.

According to Galtung's transcend perspective of conflict resolution which includes the diagnosis, prognosis and therapy elements; the Angolan civil war is diagnosed as a "resource driven war with international complicity", with "diplomatic stagnation and continued warfare" as prognosis, and finally "quiet informal diplomacy, humanitarian cease-fire, local power" are suggested for therapy.[4]

B. Civil war in Angola

The **diagnosis** element includes "ethnic, colonial and Cold War" as the origins of the conflict. In addition, structures of patronage or autocracies, which are run by small oligarchies with little or no people participation, provide the central organization. On the other hand, there is the international community support, which is focused on the government side and prohibits contact with the opposition UNITA party, though some evidence was found for CIA support for both sides. Besides, each of the major internal and external parties is seeking interests and profit from the war economy because of "the lack of governance, regulation and taxation results in corruption, high crime rates (including by the police), poverty, empty schools and the spread of infectious diseases". In addition, the electoral system, which is modelled on the US two-party system, is perceived as "very ill-matched to the complexities of Angolan society".[5]

With the end of the Cold War and the demise of the Soviet Union, the international scene witnessed a shift from interstate conflicts to other types of conflicts such as: "internal conflicts, ethnic conflicts, conflicts over secession and power struggles". Africa for instance, according to Miall et al., serves evidence for the "return of mercenary armies and underpaid militias which preyed on civilian population in a manner

---

[2] Jacob Bercovitch & Allison Houston, "The Study of International Mediation: Theoretical Issues and Empirical Evidence."
[3] H. Miall, et al., Contemporary Conflict Resolution, pp.9-13, 18
[4] J. Galtung, et al., Searching for Peace – the Road to Transcend, p.188
[5] J. Galtung, et al., op.cit., pp.297-298

reminiscent of medieval times". [6] The civil war in Angola, which started in 1975 following its independence from Portugal, is classified among the "post-colonial civil wars in which the great powers intervened as part of a continuing geopolitical struggle for power and influence". As part of new wars, the conflict in Angola bears the trait of 'war economy' which is "no longer funded by taxation and generated by state mobilization, but sustained by outside emergency assistance and the parallel economy including unofficial export of timber and precious metals, drug-trafficking, criminal rackets, plunder". Besides, this conflict also features six aspects such as "non-authority-oriented, anti-colonial secessionist, indigenous control of authority structures, external imposition of authority structures, and Cold War sponsored". [7] According to Lowe, the country was a "victim of outside interference and the Cold War" with the following states involved[8]:

- South African troops invaded Angola in support of UNITA (National Union for the Total Independence of Angola) and its leader Jonas Savimbi.
- Zaire with the US backing invasion to support of the FNLA (National Front for the Liberation of Angola) with advisers, cash and armaments, and encouraged it to attack MPLA.
- Russian weapons and the Cuban army backed the marxist MPLA and its leader Neto.
- The US thought that "joint government of FNLA and UNITA would be more amenable and open to Western influence.

Moreover, it has also been argued that "contemporary internal wars may represent the emergence of entirely new types of social formation adapted for survival on the margins of the global economy". For instance, "actors like the international drug cartels in Central and South America, the Taliban in Afghanistan and rebel groups in West Africa have effectively set up parallel economies, trading in precious resources such as hardwoods, diamonds, drugs and so on". In other words, "these wars can be seen to be both lucrative and rational for those who can take advantage and are prepared to act violently to gain power." The behaviour of these rebel groups is described as warlordism and reflects a "ruthless and extractive attitude towards society and the economy and by reliance on military force and violence". Indeed, in this case "the violence goes beyond rational expectations of what can be gained economically, for a rational warlord would not kill the goose that lays in the golden egg."[9] The con-

---

[6] ibid., p.3
[7] H. Miall, et al., op.cit., pp.69, 71
[8] N. Lowe, Mastering Modern World History, pp.537-557
[9] H. Miall, et al., op.cit., pp.130-131

tinuation of the conflict for more than twenty years following independence in 1975 revealed the failure of the three attempts to cooperate between the fighting groups. Indeed, the parties were to find it "difficult to agree on a peaceful solution that satisfies both, and find themselves locked in a Prisoner's Dilemma". In the war economy perspective, on the one hand these three unsuccessful peace agreements and the enduring conflict also suggest that Angola's "natural resources such as oil and diamonds have been of major importance in sustaining the conflict in Angola since the end of the Cold War". In this context, the revenue from oil has been of great importance for the government army in order to finance the war, as international oil companies had also shown their interest in Angola's oil and with their technology making extraction of oil possible. The size of the oil and diamond reserves was indeed decisive for the scope of the fighting. For instance, the two groups, FAA and UNITA, were to decide on the fighting effort according to "their expectations of the size of the rent". In this case, a higher rent than expected meant an increase in the fighting, i.e. war is seen as more profiting than peace; whereas a lower rent would reduce its extent. On the other hand, the conflict also reflected "a contest between the government and the rebel group over the resource rent". According to Andersen, "in both duopoly and civil war, there is competition between two parties to get the highest expected payoffs". Following this approach, the conflict in Angola actually lasted "for four decades since both FAA and UNITA want to control the whole resource rent by governing the country".[10] The persistence of the war was also due in large part from interested external parties, for instance the US.

C. The US as an interested third party

According to Miall et al., governments often "play a prominent role as mediators". However, governments are not always inclined "to shoulder a mediating role when their national interests are not at stake, and, where they are, mediation readily blurs into traditional diplomacy and statecraft". Moreover, it can also seem unavoidable that "when governments bring coercion to bear to try to force parties to change position, they become actors in the conflict." In the case of the US, due to its particular international position, it plays a significant role in post-Cold War conflicts. It is also seen as a "decisive conflict manager in many regions of the world, but there is limited domestic support for foreign interventions, and Congress remains suspicious of multi-

---

[10] http://www.prio.no/cscw/wg3/Resources%20and%20Conflict%20in%20Angola.pdf

lateral diplomacy and UN action".[11] Yet, its involvement as a third party still lies in the context of its foreign policy. According to S. Touval, mediation as part of foreign policy is "a purposive strategic behavior, a behavior motivated by a conscious calculation of advantages". It is also assumed that "domestic and foreign policy considerations do not merely motivate states to engage in mediation, but also shape the strategies and tactics of mediation". Besides, it is supposed that "a state's strategies, tactics, and goals in performing a mediation are frequently shaped by concerns external to the conflict". This assumption does not mean however that "mediating states disregard principles for effective mediation, but rather that effectiveness is usually a secondary consideration, subordinate to the mediating state's primary domestic and foreign policy concerns." In this context, the perspective of mediation as foreign policy sees mediation as a policy instrument and as such it "lends itself to comparison with other policy instruments – diplomatic (such as the construction of alliances, coalitions, and institutions), military, and economic (trade and other economic measures".[12]

In the Angolan civil war, the role of the US was dual. By supporting UNITA, it considered the war as yet "another staging ground for East-West conflict instead of as a power struggle between two groups in Angola". Its second role was that of "mediator in the search for a peaceful solution". Being on the side of Portugal, its NATO partner, the US could not support the cause for an independent Angola and was therefore to back "the foes of the Soviet-supported MPLA". However, as independence took place in 1975, the US realized it had supported the wrong party. Still, by refusing to recognize the Angolan government the US was both "hypocritical and shortsighted and allowed for a more protracted war".[13]

The backbones of US policy toward Angola at that time were non-recognition of the MPLA government and support for UNITA. Diplomatic relations are considered as "essential for orderly interactions between nations in the international arena, providing them a means for resolving problems peacefully". The use of diplomatic recognition to "express moral judgment of other political systems, especially those perceived as radical and consequently against American interest" was used by the US towards communist regimes such as the Soviet Union (1917-1933) and China (1949-1979) but also in Angola. Although the US supported the FNLA and UNITA prior to inde-

---

[11] H. Miall, et al., op.cit., pp.161, 140
[12] Saadia Touval, "Mediation and Foreign Policy"
[13] Miller Jake C., "America and the Angolan civil war"

pendence, it did not follow the international community, which included most African and Western nations in extending recognition to the newly formed government under MPLA. In these circumstances, in order to gain US diplomatic support, the Angolan government sought for Soviet assistance, so as to show the US that by backing UNITA, the US was "waging a war against the people and government of a nation that was truly dedicated to the achievement of peace and the building of a democratic state". Indeed, for the Angolan government it was difficult to understand Washington's hostility in a context where "the East-West confrontation has largely dissipated". The American position was thus seen as being "deeply contrary to the universal trend of using dialogue." Dos Santos was disappointed "over the refusal of the United States to normalize relations" and considered this great power as "more concerned with the elevation of UNITA to power than the democratization of the nation". US policy has however been consistent regarding its support for UNITA since the Reagan administration "pledged its total support for the band of 'freedom fighters' and following a globalist approach, supporting UNITA implied a message for the Soviet Union, declaring that "its adventurism in southern Africa would not be tolerated." The prospective for a UNITA victory in the civil war, according to the US, would lead to the creation a government that would meet the required US standards. On the other hand it also appears that this US policy was to "assure a military stalemate, thus forcing the two warring parties to the peace table". Ironically though, "when peace seemed to be at hand on some occasions, Washington would increase its support for UNITA." [14]

During the early stage of the war, US interest was still more in containing what it saw as "Soviet expansionism" than in resolving the civil war itself. [15] Kissinger's aim instead of winning the war was to demonstrate that "the Soviets should not be permitted to make a move in any remote part of the world without being confronted militarily by the United States." Hence the Ford administration – through the Central Intelligence Agency (CIA) — was to spend more than thirty million dollars during its 1975 anti-MPLA operations, which also included facilitating the recruitment of mercenaries." This covert assistance was designated as "non-lethal, humanitarian aid". [16] By the mid-1980, after being convinced that the Reagan administration would not further aid UNITA, Congress repealed the Clark amendment. Nonetheless, when in early

---

[14] Miller Jake C., op.cit.
[15] Miller Jake C., op.cit.
[16] Nesbitt Prexy, "US foreign policy: Lessons from the Angola conflict"

1986 Savimbi came to Washington to have recourse to US assistance, Reagan accepted and instructed the CIA to supply up UNITA with $15 million worth of arms and ammunition. Hence, despite regional peace efforts, the US continued to militarily support UNITA. And even though the Senate Intelligence Committee voted to continue the program in fiscal 1991, aid was not given any specific conditions. The reason behind was that the Bush administration hoped to show that the aim of the covert aid program was to help achieve diplomatic progress. In this context, the State Department felt "somewhat encouraged by a recent agreement between UNITA and the Angolan government, under which both sides would allow U.N.-sponsored emergency food shipments to be delivered to the estimated 250,000 civilians at immediate risk from famine". [17]

On the whole, US support of UNITA was however disregarding Angolan electoral laws which "forbid any foreign assistance to political parties". In this context, it would be later criticized that "for an administration that was able to find an estimated $75 million a year to give to UNITA in the final years of the war in Angola, the amount of money which the Bush administration is allocating for peace is grossly inadequate". Indeed, "it is apparent from the meager aid being allocated, and the continuing aid to UNITA in violation of Angolan law, that the Bush administration has yet to learn the final lesson from the Angolan conflict. Democracy is built on institutions, not on individuals".[18] Nevertheless, given the Cold War scenario, the US role in the mediation efforts was seen as inevitable because of the Soviet Union's declining influence in international affairs. Still, the position of the US, from being a major foe of Angola to become the most effective peacemaker, could be understood for instance due to the fact that although fought in Africa the conflict was not really an "African" war. Indeed, in the Cold War scenario, the two superpowers were to define "the goals of the war in terms of their interests" and then "proceeded to devote their efforts to deciding which of the two superpowers would ultimately prevail in Angola". In this manner, realizing "the strong American determination to support UNITA to the end, the Angolan government concluded that its chances of obtaining an outright victory were virtually nil" so that it was the ripe moment for a negotiated settlement. It was therefore evident that the US was the "primary peacemaker largely because of the inability of other possible mediators to function effectively". The effectiveness of the US as a peacemaker can be assigned to "its influence over one of the parties and the

---

[17] Doherty, C. J., "Wars of proxy losing favor as Cold War tensions end"

potential influence which it could exert on the other". The Angolan government thus "wanted so badly what the United States could offer that it was willing to endure the insults which had been inflicted upon it--non recognition and support of its rival UNITA--to obtain its goal."[19]

D. Conflict resolution

According to Miall et al., "civil wars ended by negotiated settlements are more likely to lead to the recurrence of armed conflicts than those ended by military victories". But conversely, "those ended by military victories are more likely to lead to genocide". The difficulty of conflict resolution also lays in the fact that "violence spawns a host of groups who benefit directly from its continuation". The civil war in Angola illustrated that for instance "soldiers become dependent on warfare as a way of life, and warlords on the economic resources and revenue they can control". Besides, as in the case of Savimbi, "leaders who have become closely identified with pursuing the conflict may risk prosecution, overthrow or even death once the war is over, and have strong incentives for intransigence".[20]

After ceasefire was declared in 1992, elections monitored by the UN took place and resulted in MPLA victory with 58% seats in parliaments and 49,57% for president Dos Santos. UNITA on the other hand won 31% seats and 40,07% for Savimbi. As somehow expected, UNITA refused to accept the result and renewed the civil war. The US was held responsible for encouraging UNITA because it has not officially recognized the MPLA until May 1993, or 6 months after UNITA had resumed the war. It was not until the ceasefire negotiation in October 1994 leading to the peace agreement a month later that UNITA was to finally accept the 1992 election result, and would play a part in the coalition government. However, Savimbi broke the terms of the agreement by financing his forces wit the proceeds from illicit sales of diamonds, to struggle against the government until his death in 2002. In 2002, new leaders of UNITA were willing to negotiate and ceasefire was signed in April 2002, with the two sides promising to keep the terms of the 1994 agreement.[21]

The dual role of the US in Angola is seen as having delayed the conflict resolution due to its support for internal disunity. Indeed, it has been suggested that there is

---

[18] Nesbitt Prexy, op.cit.
[19] Miller Jake C., op.cit.
[20] H. Miall, et al., op.cit., pp.154-155
[21] N. Lowe, op.cit., p.558

a relationship between internal unity and successful conflict resolution. Raymond and Kegley (1985) for instance state that "the greater the cultures differences between disputants, the less likelihood of successful mediation". Kressel and Pruitt (1989) in line with this argument emphasized that "internal discord within a state has a negative impact on its interactions with other states". Ott (1972) and Young (1967) on the other hand observed that "the smaller the power differences between the adversaries, the greater the effectiveness of international mediation".[22]

D.1. A Transcend perspective

Galtung's **prognosis** analysis suggests that "unless there is a break in the political stalemate, the war economy is likely to maintain violence at various levels of intensity for decades, since military resources will finance military expenditures, enriching elites in Angola and in the International Community".[23] A **therapy** therefore suggests that the "complexity of conflict must be met wit complexity of strategic peace confrontation". Indeed, "the political stalemate should be broken through a combination of (1) quiet, informal diplomacy; (2) humanitarian cease-fire for polio eradication; and (3) public information on the wealth accrual in Angolan and international elites by exploiting opportunities from the war economy". In addition, "reinvention of the public sphere should include a substantive dialogue to bring about a new electoral system with power sharing more suitable to the Angolan socio-political landscape". Moreover, "war diamonds and war oil should be monitored and (to the extent possible) traced, with diamonds addressed in the market place and oil by shareholder action."[24]

Conclusion

Indirect and direct interventions have been present throughout the interstate-intrastate conflict in Angola. According to D. Rothschild, "the actual use of combat forces is regarded as the distinguishing characteristic between the indirect and direct forms of intervention". In the case of indirect interventions, i.e. practiced by both the US and the Soviet Union, means such as "declarations of support, commitments of economic and military assistance, and covert action in favor of a particular Angolan movement or movements" were used. These two great powers, wary of the potential

---

[22] Jacob Bercovitch & Allison Houston, op.cit.
[23] J. Galtung, et al., op.cit., pp.297-298

dangers of encountering each other in combat, were to encourage the two lesser powers, i.e. South Africa and Cuba, for military intervention. Not only had these great powers "the incentives to remain indirect intervenors", but they also had "the resources at their disposal to facilitate an end to the internationalized aspects of the Angolan war".[25] It has however been suggested that Africa has never been a primary concern on the US's foreign policy agenda. In the case of Angola, the US even lacked knowledge about the Angolan nationalist movements as the National Security Study Memorandum (NSSM) 39, a major review of American policy toward southern Africa undertaken by the Nixon administration, mentioned that "African insurgent movements were ineffectual, lacked 'depth and permanence' of resolve, and did not constitute 'realistic or supportable' alternatives to continued white rule in the area". Therefore, influenced by this document, and given the context of Cold War rivalry and strategic interests, US policy toward Angola was to "encompass two mutually exclusive goals: continued expressions of sympathy with Angola's aspirations for self-determination, and the desire to give assistance to Portugal, a NATO ally that controlled the Azores air bases". The latter was ranked higher by former Secretary of State Henry A. Kissinger.

In sum, in my opinion the dual role played by the US in the conflict, as a third party peacemaker with strategic interests rendered the resolution of the conflict more difficult and led to its continuation to result in great loss of human lives.

---

[24] J. Galtung, et al., op.cit., pp.297-298
[25] D. Rothchild, op.cit.

Annex

Angola, a chronology of key events:

1300s - Kongo kingdom consolidates in the north.

Luanda: A departure point for Brazil-bound slaves Founded by Portuguese in 1567 Capital of independent Angola from 1975

1483 - Portuguese arrive.

1575 - Portuguese found Luanda.

17th and 18th centuries - Angola becomes a major Portuguese trading arena for slaves. Between 1580 and 1680 a million plus are shipped to Brazil.

1836 - Slave trade officially abolished by the Portuguese government.

1885-1930 - Portugal consolidates colonial control over Angola, local resistance persists.

1951 - Angola's status changes from colony to overseas province.

1956 - The early beginnings of the socialist guerrilla independence movement, the People's Movement for the Liberation of Angola (MPLA), based in northern Congo.

1950s-1961 - Nationalist movement develops, guerrilla war begins.

1961 - Forced labour abolished after revolts on coffee plantations leave 50,000 dead. The fight for independence is bolstered.

1974 - Revolution in Portugal, colonial empire collapses.

Independence

Up to 300,000 people died in the 27-year civil war Jonas Savimbi's Unita movement took up arms against political rivals after independence Deals in 1991 and 1994 failed to bring lasting peace Savimbi's death in 2002 heralded demobilisation of Unita fighters

1975 - Angola gains independence but power struggle ensues between MPLA, backed by Cuba, and the FNLA plus Unita, backed by South Africa and the USA.

1976 - MPLA gains upper hand.

1979 - MPLA leader Agostinho Neto dies. Jose Eduardo dos Santos takes over as president.

1987 - South African forces enter Angola to support Unita.

1988 - South Africa, Angola, Cuba sign agreement on withdrawal of Cuba's 50,000 troops from Angola by mid-1991. South African army withdraws.

1989 - Dos Santos, Unita leader Jonas Savimbi agree cease-fire, which collapses soon afterwards and guerrilla activity resumes.

Towards peace

1991 April - MPLA drops Marxism-Leninism in favour of social democracy.

1991 May - Dos Santos, Savimbi sign peace deal in Lisbon which results in a new multiparty constitution.

1992 September - Presidential and parliamentary polls certified by UN monitors as generally free and fair. Dos Santo gains more votes than Savimbi, who rejects results and resumes guerrilla war.

Peace agreement was reached without outside mediation

1993 - UN imposes sanctions against Unita. The US acknowledges the MPLA.

1994 - Government, Unita sign Lusaka Protocol peace accord.

1995 - Dos Santos, Savimbi meet, confirm commitment to peace. First of 7,000 UN peacekeepers arrive.

1996 - Dos Santos, Savimbi agree to form unity government join forces into national army.

1997 April - Unified government inaugurated, with Savimbi declining post in unity government and failing to attend inauguration ceremony.

1997 May - Tension mounts, with few Unita troops having integrated into army.

1998 - Full-scale fighting resumes. UN plane shot down. Angola intervenes in civil war in Democratic Republic of Congo on the side of President Laurent-Desire Kabila.

1999 - UN ends its peacekeeping mission.

2002 February - Savimbi killed by government troops.

2002 April - Government, Unita sign ceasefire.

Demobilisation

2002 May - Unita's military commander says 85% of his troops have gathered at demobilisation camps. There are concerns that food shortages in the camps could threaten the peace process.

2002 June - UN appeals for aid for thousands of refugees heading home after the ceasefire.

ISAIAS SAMAKUVA Election of its leader marked Unita's transition to political party

Medical charity Medecins sans Frontieres says half a million Angolans are facing starvation, a legacy of civil war.

2002 August - Unita scraps its armed wing. "The war has ended," proclaims Angola's defence minister.

2003 January - President Dos Santos appoints Fernando da Piedade Dias dos Santos, known as Nando, as prime minister. The post had been vacant for more than three years.

2003 February - UN mission overseeing the peace process winds up.

2003 June - Unita - now a political party - elects Isaias Samakuva as its new leader.

2004 April onwards - Tens of thousands of illegal foreign diamond miners are expelled in a crackdown on illegal mining and trafficking. In December the government says 300,000 foreign diamond dealers have been expelled.

2004 September - Oil production reaches one million barrels per day.

2005 March-May - Marburg virus, which is deadlier than Ebola, kills more than 300 people, most of them in the north.

References

Books

➤ N. Lowe, Mastering Modern World History, Palgrave Macmillan, 2005.

➤ H. Miall, et al., Contemporary Conflict Resolution, Blackwell Publishing Ltd, Oxford, 1999 (reprinted 2003).

➤ J. Galtung, et al., Searching for Peace – the Road to Transcend, Pluto Press, USA, 2002.

Journal articles

➤ Saadia Touval, "Mediation and Foreign Policy", *International Studies Review (2003) 5(4)*, 91–95, Paul H. Nitze School of Advanced International Studies, Johns Hopkins University.

➤ Snyder, Robert S. "The U.S. and third World Revolutionary States: Understanding the Breakdown in Relations", *International Studies Quarterly* (1999) 43 (2), 265-290.

➤ Mi Yung Yoon, "Explaining U.S. Intervention in Third World Internal Wars, 1945-1989", *Journal of Conflict Resolution*, Vol. 41, No. 4 (Aug., 1997) , pp. 580-602

➤ Nesbitt, Prexy, "US foreign policy: Lessons from the Angola conflict" in *Africa Today*, 1992 1st/2nd Quarters, Vol. 39 Issue 1/2, p53, 19p

➤ Miller Jake C., "America and the Angolan civil war", *in Transafrica Forum*, Winter 91/92, Vol. 8 Issue 4, p53, 15p

➤ Donald Rothchild, Caroline Hartzell, "Great- and Medium-Power Mediations: Angola", *Annals of the American Academy of Political and Social Science*, Vol. 518, Resolving Regional Conflicts: International Perspectives (Nov., 1991) , pp. 39-57

➤ Rothchild, Donald, Conflict management in Angola, *TransAfrica Forum*, 07308876, Spring91, Vol. 8, Issue 1

➤ Doherty, C. J., "Wars of proxy losing favor as Cold War tensions end", *Congressional Quarterly Weekly Report*, 8/25/90, Vol. 48 Issue 34, p2 721, 5p, 1 chart, 4bw

➤ "US Policy Towards Angola", *Congressional Digest*, Apr 86, Vol. 65 Issue 4, p99-128, 30p

Retrieved from the World Wide Web in April 2006

➢ http://news.bbc.co.uk/go/pr/fr/-/2/hi/africa/4872876.stm
Sarah Grainger, "War-scarred Angola seeks a future: Angola is marking four years since the government and the Unita rebels signed a peace agreement, ending 27 years of almost continuous war", BBC NEWS, April 4, 2006.

➢ http://www.usc.edu/dept/LAS/ir/cis/cews/database/SouthAfrica/southafrica.pdf
Vasu Gounden and Hussein Solomon, "Conflict Resolution in Africa: a Comparative Analysis of Angola and South Africa".

➢ http://news.bbc.co.uk/go/pr/fr/-/2/hi/africa/country_profiles/1839740.stm
Timeline: Angola, December 8, 2005.

➢ http://www.c-r.org/accord/ang/accord15/
Guus Meijer, "From military peace to social justice? The Angolan peace process", 2004.

➢ http://www.trinstitute.org/ojpcr/3_2fredpr.htm
Brian Frederking, Andrea Pyatt, and Shaun Randol, "Who You Gonna Call? Third Parties, Conflict Resolution, and the End of the Cold War", *OJPCR: The Online Journal of Peace and Conflict Resolution*, Issue 3.2, June 2000.

➢ http://www.trocaire.org/policyandadvocacy/trocairedevelopmentreview/peacebuildingangola.pdf
Róisín Shannon, "Peacebuilding and conflict resolution interventions in post-conflict Angola: NGDOs' negotiating theory and practice"

➢ http://www.prio.no/cscw/wg3/Resources%20and%20Conflict%20in%20Angola.pdf
Kirsten Hegsvold Andersen, "Resources and Conflict in Angola, An economic conflict analysis"

➢ http://www.posc.canterbury.ac.nz/staff_pages/jbercovitch/publications/intmediation.pdf
Jacob Bercovitch & Allison Houston, "The Study of International Mediation: Theoretical Issues and Empirical Evidence."